Flamingo Nation

ACKNOWLEDGEMENTS

Grateful acknowledgement to the editors of the following publications in which some of the poems in this book first appeared, often in earlier versions:

Birchsong: "Gap Road", "Hidden Country", "To the black boy who painted his arms white"

Garden Dreams CD (Aaron Marcus): "Floodwood Pond"

Himalaya Journal: "Immigrant Train, NYC"

Oberon: "Immigrant Train, NYC"

The Path to Kindness (ed. James Crews): "Floodwood Pond"

Vermont Troubadour: "Men's Group"

Earlier versions of "Above the Dental Office," "Amanita," "Flamingo Nation," "Snake Skin," "Teddi's Garden," and "Virgin Mary" first appeared in *Tasting Precious Metal, poems by Danny Dover* (Antrim House, 2014)

Onion River Press
Burlington, VT 05401
info@onionriverpress.com
www.onionriverpress.com

ISBN: 978-1-957184-57-9

Library of Congress Control Number: 2024907482

Flamingo Nation

new and selected poems
Danny Dover

ONION RIVER PRESS

BURLINGTON, VERMONT

ALSO BY DANNY DOVER

Tasting Precious Metal (Antrim House, 2014)

Kindness Soup, Thankful Tea (chapbook, 2006)

Special thanks to:

Rolf Olsen, layout and design

David Powell, cover graphics and design

My gratitude to Don Collins, Eric Webb, James Crews, and dozens of friends and readers for their encouragement over these many years.

Many thanks to Janet Watton and the folks at PoemTown Randolph.

I'm very grateful to both Aaron Marcus and Dorothy Robson for their beautiful piano compositions inspired by many of the poems.

And to my wife, Mary, for her love, support, and sound judgement when, as often is the case, she's the first reader of a new poem!

TABLE OF CONTENTS

PROLOGUE

Poems are everywhere

when times get hard
because when times get hard
poems are everywhere
to be found   the drumbeat
from pelting rain
like a troubled heart
that never stops

We search for words
under the words
when times get hard
like starving deer
in drifting snow
pawing for apples
at winter's end

A Country of Delight

It's good to know
that somewhere
in this hardened world
there's still a country
where motorways are
moved for fairy trees

And when a rare blizzard
lays a level blanket
over every city
farm and village
suspending normal
life for days and days
the stores sell out
of carrots
for thousands of families
rushing out to build
the only snowmen
of their lives

And though this alone
may never heal the world
of every sorrow
sown for centuries
it's proof at least
of the boundless joy
just waiting underground
for the perfect moment
to burst the surface
of our longing
for a country of delight

County Cork, Ireland

Above the Dental Office

From school each day
I'd return to a room
above the office
of my dentist father
over the piercing whine
of molars filled
and whimpering pleas
of children trapped
like cornered animals
and my father's voice
so caring and calm
and soothing as mint
drifting up through
ceiling cracks
with strains of muzak
in a muted soundtrack
for coming of age
during warm afternoons
of salacious groping
with a chain-smoking
girlfriend who soon
would leave me alone
in despair scorned for spitting
each time I French-kissed
her full luscious mouth

Disgust and desire
and the shriek of the drill
all throbbing together
in the air of a room
where I first learned
it's possible
to live with pain
or at least lie down
just a few feet above it

Accident

(for L.)

We are total strangers
yet here it is
a hospital room
with not enough chairs
and a missing leg
yours torn like paper
from your body

Maybe you glimpsed
Mary's blooming gardens
as you cruised by
moments before time stopped
sufficient reason
to be here now
flowers gripped by hands
ill at ease in this room
of phantom limbs
I would rather hold
my breath if it could
restore you

Is this what it takes?
A thousand miles from home
you and your husband
like two birds gently saved
from the side of our road

Spare the pity
In this world teeming
with damaged souls
we are all one tribe
circling the fire
of a new friendship
with laughter and stories
around your bed

The healing bones
know exactly what to do

Amanita

Nearly crushing her
raucous yellow umbrella
during a chilly walk
Amanita's freckled face
beaming with dew
in crisp brown field grass
This same ground in June
blushing with a feast
of ripe wild strawberries

The smallest bite
brings death or ecstasy
warns a friend
as sometimes
a few words from you
can burst underfoot
full of dread or promise
savored on the tongue
or swallowed hard

Ancient Road

A town committee at wood's edge
out to search a disputed road
now called ancient
old maps   new owners
borders drawn
volunteers and neighbors
laughing at stories
marveling at deer yards
crisp smell of fall
screech of jays
a bright blue morning
ripe and promising

A shout from somewhere
deep in a glade
The road ran here
a mud-rutted track
some assorted stones
a round of handshakes
home by noon

It could be this easy
finding the way
from here to there
from where we came
and how to move on
no guns in sight

Animal Behavior

A clever crow
coaxes a tethered dog
in circles tight
around a post
until the rope
is too short
to reach its food
then calmly feasts
while the furious canine
snarls and rages
inches away

Something familiar
in this tale
of hunger and deceit
and a rope   yes   always a rope
too short and someone
in a room upstairs
on the losing end
coiled and full
of venom
without the sense
to turn around
and slowly unravel
what's already done

At the Diner

The old tired animal in me
finds weekly respite
in this calm warm nest
perched on a stool
eyes closed   fresh coffee
voices adrift like
an orchestra tuning
the waitress explaining
her tattoo between refills
a long graceful curving vine
of leaves and constellations
for each of the loving people
in her life spiraling around
and up her smooth young limb
and for a moment
I see myself on that vine
or any one of a thousand others
aging my way clear up
to the thinnest of branches
before letting go

Borders

We are little nations
you and I
passing on the freeway
I welcome you the way
I welcome the sun
onto porous skin
the way my mouth opens
for a meal that delights
and sustains me
You borrow the air
from the breath
of my ancestors
Your children play
in the sandbox
of my dreams
Look at the house
we are building together
From space it floats
in a marbled glow
borderless

By the Numbers

There's comfort
I confess in living life
by the numbers
by the ebb and flow
of calories and seasons
cataloguing memories
like baseball cards
calibrating time in obituaries
measuring health in heartbeats
security in dollars

But by day's end
things never quite add up
and at night   bewildered
by the infinity of stars
I dream again
of wandering a world
beyond numbers and formulas
without any scores
to settle or keep

Chain   *(for S.)*

The father she never knew
chose instead to binge on beer
alone in a shed behind the barn
swore at anyone or anything
that moved or didn't
night after night
collecting bottle caps
like broken promises
pierced and strung
and linked in loops
in a family line
of well-kept secrets
grown longer
as she grew wiser

Sometimes forgiveness
can break a chain
over a stretch of decades
like fresh paint on a rusted relic
sprayed glossy gold
a father's lineage
hung out to dry
gleaming in the warmth
of her backyard garden

Coffin

My friend's grandfather
a buddhist who felt
his time was near
built a coffin in the kitchen
set on sawhorses to settle in
and get comfortable
sleeping there every night
for two months but then got better
so the coffin was stored away
and frankly I'm no different
with a coffin or two
of my own in the attic
but sooner or later
it's time to clean house
so there you are
in the dim light and spider webs
with a box full of old letters
and before you know it
you've lain down
in those dusty words
and passed from here
into another world

Collisions

A distracted teen
driving to school
strikes a classmate
crossing the street

Decades later
they meet again
one a stunt-man
the other a surgeon

Imagine the screech of brakes
thud of a body
flying through space
textbooks scattering
flutter of pages
smell of cut grass
and burning rubber

One floating by
amazed to be airborne
the other staring
through shattered glass
eyes meeting
in a future puzzle
solved only with a piece
from the life of another

In a risky collision
radio blasting
windows down
a blinding glint
of morning sun

Crooked Gravity

Even as
my chiropractor claims
there is no symmetry
somewhere a woman
slips on a ring
eager to take a vow
while another   betrayed
removes her ring
to a dusty drawer
love   grief
and crooked gravity
meandering
through the limbs
of each aging body
grown lopsided
and beautiful

Day #27,072

To the lady selling Asian greens
The baker downtown with cowboy cookies
Ripening blueberries
A bright red male cardinal on the wood pile
The man who cuts my firewood
Sheets of rain and clear sky afterward
Steam rising from hot pavement
Heat pumps and radar and internet
Late afternoon light
Summer porches and cats
Two dozen utility workers in the late-night storm
The cashier at Shaws
My tired willing body
Rare earth minerals
and stone walls and buddha statues
Fireflies and flowers and friends
Poetry and music but mostly music
The inventor of clothes pins
Boredom and love
and lawnmowers
and the lawnmower repair guy
and the kid who helps him
Mystery and awe
Clean socks
Water and air

Dear Planet

Look we didn't mean it things just got out of hand   I mean honestly what could you expect from a bunch of fourteen-year-olds   you leave a big beautiful house like that with the door unlocked a fridge full of cold beer and all the pizza we could eat   I admit it we wrecked the place   But what a party   Sorry about the smashed furniture and all the noise   The kitchen fire was a freak accident   Someone found a key to the truck and really messed up the lawn   Don't know how the basement flooded or about that hole in the roof but we'll pay for it all I promise   Just give us another chance whatever it takes   We were jerks   Give us time to grow up settle down raise families   Our kids will behave better   I just know they will   I know they will

Flamingo Nation

Not long ago in dead
of winter a lost flamingo
turned north and tumbled
from the sky over Siberia
a shivering pink body
on spindly legs found
by startled villagers

an exotic spectacle
they bundled in furs
nursed with nettles
and warm yak milk
through sub-zero nights
by a spruce-fired stove
and restored to health
for the hard journey home

Our own flamingo beams
from a bare-limbed maple
in bright plastic exile
below the meadow
where it snagged
in flood waters
early last fall
a welcome break

from the dull winter palette
of unease and isolation
that has settled upon us
once again
when darkness portends
whatever shifting course
is feared the most
as if an entire nation

tired and lost
just dropped from the sky
without compass or map
a colorful alien creature
waiting to be thawed out
with a little kindness
and sense of direction

Floodwood Pond

Before a shattered world
can begin to heal
it might first float here
amid moss and minnows
in the shimmering mist
of an approaching dawn

We have only this body
and only one earth
made from flesh and blood
of porous mountains
where a doubtful heart
may soak in warm
uncertainty

You could stay awhile
with breath and gravity
your only guides
a primal sound
pooling and rising
from somewhere deep
within your belly

And if you pray to stars
then here is the infinite
dance of light
upon a shrine
of rippling water

Gap Road

Driving the road
so rarely open
this late in November
to the top of the ridge
for a hike to Sunset Ledge
perched three thousand feet
above the Champlain basin
spread out for miles
like a mental problem
worth solving

Nothing much
on my horizon these days
bills paid   wood in   wife happy
gray bristled hills folded in cloaks
of stiff bare hardwoods
Far below on a clean-scrubbed
patch of dry brown farmland
one lone tractor sputtering
like a cranky old man

Soon this road shuts for winter
and some bewildered
GPS-bound traveler
will brake to a stop
just short of his goal
a feeling I know too well
not so much the getting lost
as surprise
in knowing exactly
where I am

Gathering Sheep

Coming to rest
in a well-grazed pasture
tucked deep and high
in a rugged draw
Kerry's grim-fogged
mountains leering down
with grizzled chins
of broken boulders
upon the neat-trimmed
silent long green
valley of Bridia
just a hint of rain
and nothing a-stir

A mile below
two black collies
sprint graceful arcs
the sheep as one single
fluid thing alive
and shifting
like the mind of a child
or a school of fish
darting about
then stretched wide
like rising bread
a string of pearls
strewn upon a settled land
as the earth and all
its gentle creatures
take time to play
and dance together

Co. Kerry, Ireland

Geese

A forest glade
has gifts to offer
even in November's
gloom as you rest
a moment on a rock
the one cloaked in moss
the color of the sea
where you sit
in swirling curtains
of a snow squall
listening to invisible geese
honk their hurry-ups
toward open water
and to the beech limbs
stirring like rustled
fabric felt long ago
a loose satin blouse
that once sent you
soaring

Green-up Day, 2023

Brand-new barbie dolls
abandoned by
a mountain road
on the same day
'he' testifies
'she' wasn't his 'type'

Imagine trash—
ok   let's talk trash

Or kindness—
to be found again
lifted gently
limb by limb

Someone new
somewhere
one more life
tossed away

Was a childhood lost
or was it found?

Hear their stories

Make them whole again

Hallowed Ground

When the flood
washed through the cemetery
some remains got mixed
into the bridge repair fill
so the highway crew is back
clawing through sanctified soil
salvaging what's left
for a dignified burial
up on the hill

Bless them all
for such sensitivity
but please
don't feel the need
to handle me just so
once my body and I part ways
discarded like a dried-out pod
gone to breath   stardust
and pavement

Today I'm driving
across the bones
of a thousand generations
inhaling their dust
Let me dissolve into the truck tire
Let weary hikers lounge
on my calcified bedrock
Let dolphins swim in my salts
and my minerals color the paint
in someone's future
masterpiece

Let this fragile planet
be my hallowed ground

He died instantly

drones a commentator
about someone's end
as if to say
a witness watched
the finish line crossed
before the race
had even begun
like a life squeezed
to the vanishing point
quick as the flash
of a camera
in a quiet cafe
where you sit near
a lithe young model
posing for a photo shoot
at the next table
as if you're not there

Hidden Country

Awake at first light
slipping the kayak into smooth
warm water   skimming
through pre-dawn fog toward
subtle movements in the reeds
a slow and silent drift
within a paddle's length
of a well-shielded beaver clan
offspring whining like spoiled pups
nibbling fresh green shoots
tsch   tsch   tsch
so faint it barely breaks
the tender core of this soundless
hour before the earth takes
its first deep breath

Tonight at dinner
three choppers
from a nearby base
roar in so loud
and low across the lake
I crouch for cover
TUK-TUK-TUK-TUK
they chew up bits
of sky and disappear

Home Depot

The thoughtful ones
who ply these paths
mutter to themselves
in deep concentration
reciting lists
like silent prayers
amid stacks of lumber
and bulging bins
of cotter pins
and carriage bolts
in search of the key
to a puzzle
only they understand
in a world that's always
needed fixing
by those who've known
to listen like shamans
for benevolent spirits
in steel wool and drill bits
sharp flint and firm fiber
the rich dense forest
teeming with tools
whispering whispering
Use us! Use us!

Hummingbirds

Sipping scotch
on the neighbor's porch
watching hummingbirds
sparring like fighter jets
as he recalls coaching
the year the girl
with cigarette burns
and a hair-trigger temper
tries out for the team
like some feral animal
but boy
could she rebound

So for one big season
those small-town girls
are the family
she never knew
and together
with a furious flutter
of little wings
claw their way
clear up to All-State

Hunger Mountain, 1816

Whoever named this mountain
in the year of Eighteen-hundred-
and-froze-to-death
knew a thing or two
of empty bellies
swelled with rumors
and rotting corn
as the weakened sun
shunned frozen fields

But when a crop of churches
sprouted from the fears
of forsaken souls
he alone chose instead
this rugged pinnacle
brimming with balsam fir
and sweep of falcons
over any other promise
of salvation

Jang Chu

I'm on a mountain trail with a monk
who is always happy
gently guiding worms in danger
off the path
Good he smiles
Jang Chu knows just one word
in English
Good sipping water
Good flirting with a girl he meets
Good snapping selfies with
stray dogs and curious children
Even sick and dizzy
on this treacherous walk
Jang Chu is good
All is good   but I know better
Not bad   I say
tasting the snack he offers
Good   he grins

Gorkha, Nepal

Immigrant Train, NYC

The Queens-bound subway
known as Number Seven
boards deep in a dusty cave
below Manhattan's glossy
mountains gathering
speed on screeching rails
beneath a tidal river
and bursting out into
brilliant sunlight like a well-
kept secret boldly revealed
as you ride and ride
hardly noticed
for your pale dull skin
amid a pressing mass
of faces gleaming every shade
of black or brown like polished
driftwood saved from shores
of a hundred nations

This is their ship
of gambled dreams
a pack of pilgrims
swaying over
shifting ground
in a lurching vessel
laden with all we've been
or shall become   twisting
on an ancient track
across the swirl and sprawl
of flim-flam streets
and asphalt rooftops
they now call home

John the hermit

This is how spring
arrives one morning
hitching down the road
first time since fall
missing half his teeth
and reeking of tobacco
so you pull over
give him a ride
let him unravel
a string of tall tales
with a wide-mouthed grin
that warms your heart
while a weary landscape
waits to catch a lift
from sunbeams creeping
up the frozen valley
and there you are
leaning out a window
greeting the sweet
damp smell of soil
like a long-lost friend

Journey

You pray softly
with the first taste
of sea

Vowels flutter
like colored moths
from the mouth

of a waitress
with neon hair
A ballad of stone

weighs on your heart
One fitful night
you watch until dawn

from an ancient tower
for medieval invaders
A single journey

may never conquer
such dreams
The lost luggage

bulging with weeds
is never found
Sooner or later

a stranger asks
where you come from

Kitchen

When you and I die
imagine Heaven as the kitchen
where we gather again
Forget the other rooms
with their dusty books
and packed suitcases
Heaven is warm and steamy
a slow-cooked stew
fresh-brewed coffee
gossip with neighbors
drop-ins welcome
always an empty seat
a few   a thousand
enough for all
old enemies
holding hot mugs
trading recipes
Forget the rain pounding
on the window
Make room for the refugees
with their stories full-bellied
in the knowing

Prayers like these
sustain me now
still simmering faintly
somewhere in the world

Kora at Boudha Stupa

Drawn like a moth
to the heat of this place
of prayers at dawn
a churning hub
of incense and intention
butter lamps and drum beats
beggars and believers
rotating with the earth
tilting her axis toward
the infinite promise
of an unfolding day

Boudha, Nepal

Men's Group

Gathered in the cloister
of a cluttered wood shop
minds sharp as saw teeth
eager to fix anything
other than personal flaws
passed around the room
like samples of failed
glue joints until
one hand drifts
into a bulging box
of odd-sized pine
and maple too short
or too thin or too narrow
for any practical purpose
each man finding
a choice piece
to build and balance
higher and higher
one discarded scrap
propped upon another
like vexing problems
perched over their
shaky solutions
forming a wildly
impermanent
towering display
of the fragile
messy beautiful
and somewhat
superfluous lives
of aging men

Making Plans

My father taught me
Always have a Plan A
and a Plan B

But too young for plans
I dreamed instead
of twin-lettered houses
hiding deep in A's peaked attic
or gazing out B's stacked
windows at a landscape
still beyond my vocabulary

A lifetime later
of running through
the alphabet
I know now my father
had it almost right
Everything has a plan
even moles with
their transparent trails
under crusted snow
or my once thick hair
planning a tactical retreat

Maybe there's
a language of plans
a way to sort
letters into words
and words into conversation
like the time I tried hitching
to Cranberry Portage
peeking through the zipper
of a pair of shorts
over my head
thwarting swarms
of Manitoba mosquitoes
with dusk approaching
on an empty road
and Plan B whispering
whispering softly
almost understood

Mothball Fleet, 1965

Two hundred rusted
warships strung along
a quiet stretch
of Hudson shore
purged of deadly
cargo   bellies filled
with surplus wheat
for fighting famine
anchors bound
in sunken rows
of river sludge

where we whoop
and laugh on water skis
through shadowed
gaps   cringing under
stark gray bows
in nervous dread
of drifting near
the slimy hulls

A harmless thrill
on carefree days
throttling through
a teenage summer

skimming light
as beetles
over murky water
never looking
below the surface

gripping tight
but never grasping
how short the
times can be
between dark
and looming
passages of war

Nubri

Walking with Nyima
on a thin steep line
a tightrope crossing
the treacherous face
of landslide scree
senses alert
for loosened rock

For days we've traced
the valley's vein
of seething river
clambering over
shifting ground
while here and there
beneath our feet
buried houses
return to soil

Life here is liquid
with nowhere to run
when the ground
turns to mercury
and boxcar boulders
pour down like coins
the mountain's skin
bruised and raw
peeling away
in a canyon carved
by ancient waters
rounded river stones
hugging walls
of a cliff-edged
trail at 12,000 feet

Far below
a village awaits
the approaching
highway   a new kind
of earthquake
coming soon

Gorkha, Nepal

Oh, My Heart

After two billion beats
(do the math)
and still counting
I no longer have
the heart to complain
about right or wrong
or high beams in my face
about sea levels rising
or stock markets falling
when reminded
of the miracle
of this playful puppy
within my chest
who never ceases
leaping for a ball
over and over
again and again
never tired
of showing off
his one precise
impeccable trick
with undying loyalty
begging for attention
but ignored by me
until this moment
like a slumbering old fool
who wakes in a theater
midway through the show
and jumps on a chair
screaming *encore*
encore bravo bravo

Quik Stop

Staggering through
the sliding doors
at the Thruway Quik Stop
hungry travelers desperate
for the perfect fuel
stalking crowded aisles
stuffed with stacks
of energy bars and
junk food drinks
cheezy chips
and candied nuts
Slim Jims   Kit Kats
dazzling displays
of Doodle-this
and Snicker-that
and for a moment
I could be in church
surrounded by congregants
mumbling labels
of fat and sugar content
droning from every corner
like chants or prayers
or confessions
of guilt and desire
as if we might
all be in this together
running on empty
and though not a believer
I'm also searching for
nothing less than
a source of happiness
or an end to suffering
hopeful that if only
I look long enough
the answer could be
here and now
but more likely
at the following exit

Razan al-Najjar, 1998-2018

Where was I
the day you were born?
Forgive me
for not remembering
from a corner
of the world
without snipers
Here the walls
are piles of stone
lining fields of sheep
What does
the bullet feel
piercing a heart
like yours
pouring blood into
the ground you loved?
Your life was a poem
crushed and thrown away

We prayed for rain
the day you died
Some prayers
are answered

Serang

When a child asks
Where are you from?
in the language of Kutang
a-me-rica means
gone to the hills to take a shit
a coincidence of phonemes
rolled off the tongue
like waterfalls running
down and through
every cleft of this valley
of double meanings
Here a holy well awaits you
dripping from the mouth
of a forest cliff
and a Rinpoche
dressed for royalty
runs to his kitchen
lost in the search
to serve you tea
Glaciers like ghosts
hover above where
ancient scrolls lie
buried under boulders
and wild deer tread grass
together with monks
in a place
with no way out
but only in   only in
where there can be
no map and the impossible
blue of sky may be all
that saves you

Gorkha, Nepal

Shaving in Bhaktapur *(for Urche)*

One day a fatherless boy
asks a man with no son
how to shave
the first wild sprouts
crowding his chin

So the man
unfolds his traveled face
a well-creased map
to guide the boy
on a timeless path
of steel and skin
tracing the journey
that joined them
here in a cramped room
of a crumbling hotel
in an ancient town
where crowds of men
in drunken mayhem
pull a ten-ton chariot
of ropes and timber
adorned with marigolds
and drenched with blood
to praise the gods

Biskah Jatra Festival, Nepal

Snake Skin

A snake skin
is only a snake skin
until given to the ten-year-old
who has barely begun
to trust in you

He too may shed
some doubts
like translucent scales
from his troubled heart

And peel you too
with his searching look
back to something
forgotten but true
in nature's fragile design
held weightless
and shimmering
in his restless young eyes

Some day you pray
with grace and ease
you both may shed
these clumsy skins
in tall lush grass
and slip away

Snoino

I'm studying the label
on a bag of onions
snoino spelled backwards
which reminds me
of my old Rambler
that only ran in reverse
and soon I'm in a parallel
universe where chopping snoino
makes me laugh instead of cry
and where all moments
when I meant yes
instead of no
lie waiting in a pile
like left-over parts
from a broken transmission

Which is to say
there are a few things
I would gladly reverse
if given the chance
such as poisoned words
once thrown in your face
spelled backwards now
harmless syllables
frozen in the frigid air
between us
to sprinkle down
like laughter
upon the dance floor
of our marriage

Spelling Lesson

In second grade
some girls would
lift their skirts
when the teacher
left for a smoke
a game of daring
in random flashes
around the room
like fireflies
or mollusks
moored to desks
snapped open
with rapid swooshes
inviting a glimpse
by bewildered boys
of cotton briefs
with printed patterns
of penguins piglets
and teddy bears
again and again
the Italians
always best at this
girls with names
like cheese or pasta
or secret codes
spelled out slowly
tramaglini   scazzafava
amicola   feminella

Such Women as These

These women
laughing so as they work
shrouded in scarves
from choking dust
up to their elbows
in wet cement
hauling baskets
of sand to the waiting
men   always the men
who lay brick and stone
for a burgeoning city

Women such as these
were made to last

They will outlive
the fragile men
and their flimsy walls

And at festival time
they'll wash and oil
lustrous hair
pry sand
from under crusty nails
preen pencil-thin eyebrows
polish jewelry
adorn their scented bodies
with satin saris
of astonishing color
and stride through
crowded city streets
like gleaming stars
from a distant galaxy

Kathmandu, Nepal

Teddi's Garden *(for T. P.)*

The MRI reveals how
your body now tends
a wild and strange garden
thriving tendrils
taking root in brain cells
that sowed a lifetime
of devotion
to all living things

Such fertile soil
as if cancer flowers

And could it be
otherwise?

Love like this
has no boundaries

To the black boy who painted his arms white

in the all-white school
of our all-white village
I'm pondering today
how it felt to be you
the only stroke of black
on an all-white canvas
vanishing limb by limb
wondering if you still
white-wash your dreams
still wear your shirt sleeves long
Once when things fell apart
I tried painting my heart black
and had no more use for arms
You could have mine now
they're good for holding on
I too have wished to be un-made
prayed to pass for something I'm not

Under the Aegis of High Pressure

Barely awake I hear the forecast
and already feel the peculiar
lightness of a day proceeding
with regal protection
breathing easier
now that all stress
has vanished under
the Aegis of High Pressure

Today my path glides
through traffic snarls
faucets stop leaking
bank accounts overflow
wars recede   glaciers grow
aging skin glows
pink without carcinomas
and memory rides
a bullet train
to every stop
exactly on time

Who can tell how long
this freedom may last
as we spread wings
preen feathers
feel the soft massage
of air underfoot
the tentative release
to float like hawks
toward a wild
and fearless
purpose

Virgin Mary

Her favorite figurine
now a sad pile of broken
blue-and-white porcelain
heaped on the counter
and my wife implores
a resurrection be performed
by me   a simple Jew
armed only with super glue
and trepidation
but setting mind and jaw
squarely to the task
of all mankind
I do manage restoring
her slightly-cracked
sly smile
to its proper place
the same smile
that smashed me open
more than thirty years ago
still thrilling in random glances
over a sandwich or pillow

And though we've been broken
a few times as may happen
to most things brittle
when hit by something hard
the scattered china
always beckons us
to the bare floor
on bent knees
searching eye-to-eye
under chair and table
for the missing piece
with jagged hands
sparkling blue-and-white
and soft in prayer

Wild Atlantic Way

White-knuckled and tired
we duck into a dim-lit pub
for chowder and bread
near a silent couple
who linger in a corner
staring down at half-eaten
meals   she twirls a fork
he stirs a long-forgotten coffee
something heavy hanging
in the air between
these two young natives
descendants of peasants
chieftains   pirates
and patriots
close to the edge
of some kind of reckoning

Driving on in silence
thoughts adrift
past treacherous cliffs
around hidden coves
guarding ancient ghosts

She's pregnant   you say
He's had an affair   I say

Through millennia of wars
famines   invasions
betrayals   epiphanies
lost at sea

Co. Kerry, Ireland

ABOUT THE AUTHOR

Danny Dover is a retired piano technician living in Bethel, Vermont. His poems have appeared in numerous journals, anthologies, and two previously published books: *Tasting Precious Metal* and *Kindness Soup, Thankful Tea*.